Giants on the Road

Tractor-Trailers

Norman D. Graubart

PowerKiDS press
New York

Published in 2015 by The Rosen Publishing Group, Inc.
29 East 21st Street, New York, NY 10010

First Edition

Editor: Katie Kawa
Book Design: Reann Nye

Photo Credits: Cover, p. 22 Jetta Productions/Iconica/Getty Images; pp. 5, 6 Richard Thornton/Shutterstock.com; p. 9 Gines Romero/Shutterstock.com; p. 10 R Carner/Shutterstock.com; p.13 Maxim Blinkov/Shutterstock.com; p. 14 Chad McDermott/Shutterstock.com; p. 17 Mark Yuill/Shutterstock.com; p. 18 Maria Dryfhout/Shutterstock.com; p. 21 Steve Design/Shutterstock.com.

Library of Congress Cataloging-in-Publication Data

Graubart, Norman D., author.
Tractor-trailers / Norman D. Graubart.
pages cm. — (Giants on the road)
Includes index.
ISBN 978-1-4994-0221-6 (pbk.)
ISBN 978-1-4994-0224-7 (6 pack)
ISBN 978-1-4994-0219-3 (library binding)
1. Tractor trailer combinations—Juvenile literature. I. Title.
TL230.15.G737 2015
629.224—dc23

2014025261

Manufactured in the United States of America

CPSIA Compliance Information: Batch #CW15PK: For Further Information contact Rosen Publishing, New York, New York at 1-800-237-9932

Contents

Tractor-trailers carry goods all over the country!

CARRIER

Tractor-trailers are also called semis. Some people call these trucks big rigs.

A tractor-trailer has two parts.
The tractor pulls the **trailer**.

trailer
tractor

The tractor is a machine
that can pull heavy loads.

Trailers hold goods, such as food. Some hold other things you would buy in a store.

ЛЮСТРА
3400/S

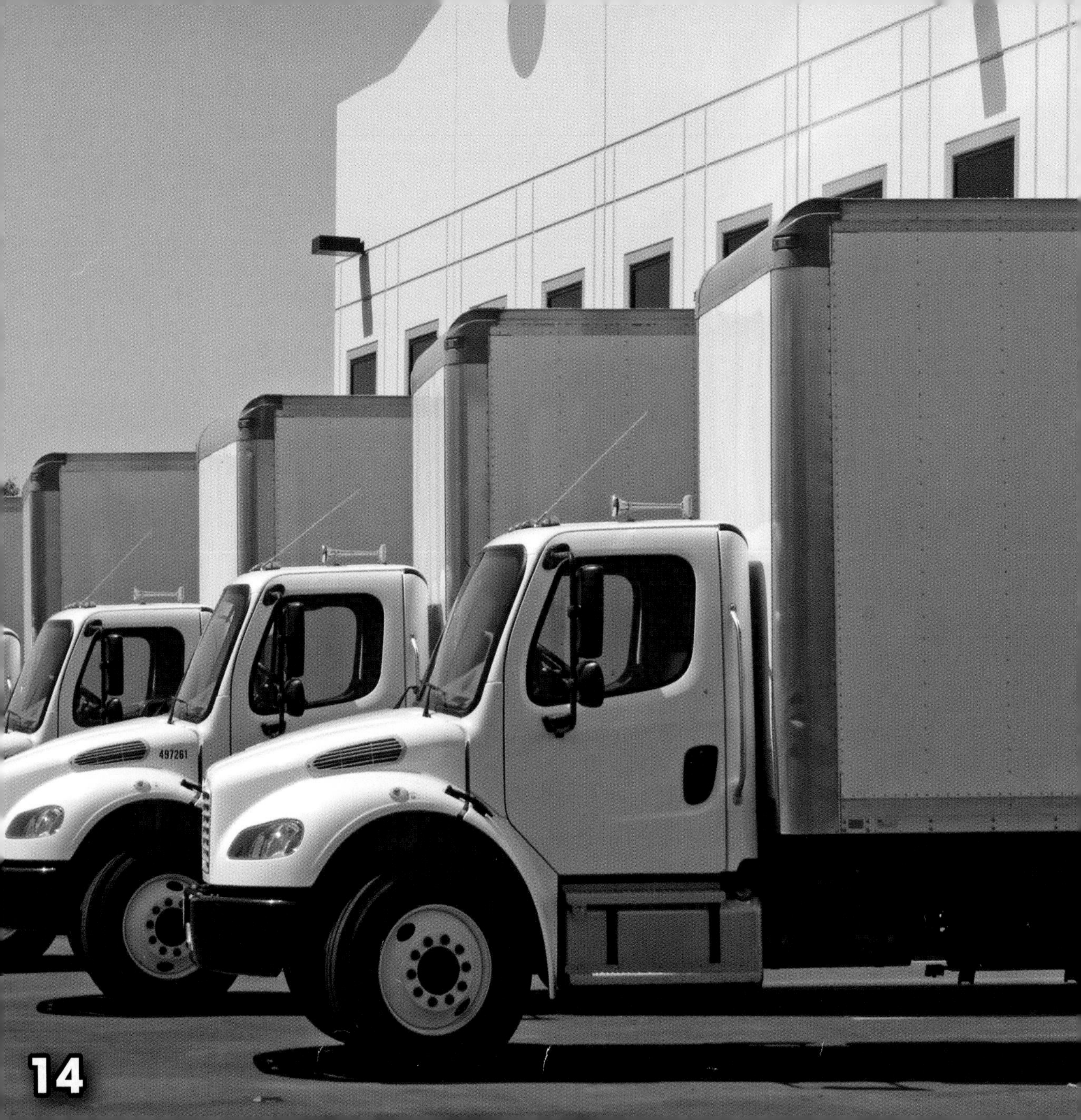
497261

A box truck carries dry goods, such as clothes or paper.

Some tractor-trailers carry food and keep it cold.

17

Flatbed tractor-trailers carry big things, such as cars and **lumber**.

Other tractor-trailers carry milk and gasoline. They're called tanker trucks.

Try to count the wheels on the next tractor-trailer you see!

Words to Know

lumber

trailer

Index

Websites

Due to the changing nature of Internet links, PowerKids Press has developed an online list of websites related to the subject of this book. This site is updated regularly. Please use this link to access the list: www.powerkidslinks.com/gotr/tract